MW01492362

YOU DESERVE YOUR OWN LOVE TOO

Poetry & Prose

CHELSEY ARMFIELD

This book is for the person who finds it easy to love others but struggles to love themself.

You deserve your own love too.

CONTENTS

LEARNING TO EMBRACE ALL OF YOU

You are so much more than your accomplishments. You are a feeling, healing, heart-beating soul whose value never perishes. Your worth can't be measured by a job, a title, a relationship, or an award. You should celebrate your wins, *but it's surely not where your worth begins.*

You deserve to be at peace with yourself. With how you show up in this world. With who you are deep down. With who you are *when no one else is around.*

What if you just plant flowers where you are now?
In the uncertainty, in the mess, in the overwhelm.
What if you let your life brim with fresh starts anyhow?

In a world of jagged cement,
be soft silk.

You don't need to perform, achieve, or impress others to be seen or to be worthy of love. Find the people who reflect this truth back to you—because love is your birthright, *not* something to fall short of.

When you see a butterfly flying alone with nothing but the golden sunrays grazing its back, you don't think, *They must be lonely.* You think of peace and transformation, a special glimpse of beauty—of flying free. I want you to know it can be the same for you. Being alone does not have to signify misfortune or an indication that you lack worth. It can mean the same thing: *peace, transformation, a special glimpse of beauty—of flying free.*

What if you learned to love the experiences that have shaped you? Not because they were pleasant or because they were indicative of what you deserved—but because they made you into the lovely human you are today. What if those trials and tribulations were predestined opportunities for soul growth? What if they were never meant to keep you stuck, but were instead meant to propel you *forward?*

Never water yourself down or customize your traits to please others. This is blatant self-betrayal. Genuine connection is knowing that someone loves and embraces you for *you* and not some fake portrayal.

Remember: it's better to be rejected for who you *are* than to be loved for who you *aren't*.

Who are you when you aren't "on"
for everyone else?

Get to know her,
cherish her,
befriend her.

The goal is to walk hand in hand with your inner child. Learn about their fears, their hopes, their dreams, and their inner voids so you can pour into them with a nurturing sense of compassion. The goal is to remember that when we are harsh on ourselves, we are actually exacting that harshness onto *them*. Let this motivate you to move through life with a more gentle, self-loving approach—it is from there, *all your healing will stem*.

Whatever you do, never punish yourself for your imperfections and perceived shortcomings. You are belittling yourself for the very nature of being human—for simply being alive. Life is full of challenges, and the last thing you need is to flood your mind with self-hatred and judgment. You are simply doing your best, *and for that* you should be nothing short of impressed.

You'll know you've reached a new level of *peace* when you are more concerned about what you are doing in life than comparing your life to anyone else's—because being in alignment with *self* is what true wealth is.

The world has convinced you that when they clap, you are succeeding. But it's often the quiet, personal goals that are the worthiest of celebration. So by all means—*give yourself* the standing ovation.

Who you are is a work of art: layered, unique, valuable, expressive, and full of contrasting traits. Your life's history has shaped who you are today, like brush strokes on a canvas, or hands molding a sculpture. You are one of a kind, an original. And much like art, you are ever-evolving. In your *trauma*, there is room for resilience and healing. In your *insecurity*, there is room for self-love and self-assurance. In your *imperfections*, there is room for radical self-acceptance. In your *complacency*, there is room for an intentionally romanticized life. In your *deep-rooted fear*, there is room to comfort your inner child. In your *rushing*, there is room for a slow, soft life rooted in trust. *You are a work of art*: finished in the sense of your inherent wholeness, and unfinished in the sense of your boundless potential to become whoever you wish to be in this world.

Don't be fooled by this world and what it chooses to celebrate most—there is nothing more precious than a pure heart with pure intentions.
You are a rare gem in human form.

You can't hate yourself into becoming who you want to be. Self-hatred is a confined cage, and self-love is the only key to set you *free*.

Don't ever count yourself out just because others have. *You are brimming with potential.* Anyone who tries to convince you otherwise is further proof why *self-belief is essential.*

Your life will change drastically when you take all the time you spent comparing your life to others and instead, invest it in appreciating the intricacies of the life you're currently living.

We're taught that having more will translate to feeling better, but this isn't true. Feeling better is an inside job, *made possible only by you.*

You are not the pain and trauma you've experienced. And you are not the damaged goods you often feel like. You came to this earth as a pure soul comprised with nothing but love and light, and this will forever and always be your birthright. So don't let this world trick you into thinking you are broken down or past your prime, or that you missed out in this lifetime.

Remember, a flower's likelihood of growing and flourishing is much greater when in a spacious bed of soil than in a crowded bed of smothering weeds. So if you have to be alone for a bit, at least you know you are in fertile grounds, free to *expand and grow* in leaps and bounds.

Whatever you do, don't spend your life chasing after someone else's approval, especially when, deep down, they don't even approve of themself.

Some days you will meditate, journal, go for a walk, and hydrate, yet it still won't feel like enough. You will feel at odds within your body, within this world, and you will question everything. And everything will feel hard. Like a storm in the night, catching you completely off guard. But please remember this feeling won't last. And this certainly won't be the foreseeable forecast. It's a short moment, a bad day, something you will soon file away. But for now, remember to tell your inner child, *"It will all be okay."*

We search for wisdom in books, guru's, and workshops—but we seldom remember there is wisdom found *in and all around us.*

When you do things for your own approval rather than anyone else's, that's when you know you are living in alignment—the very moment when you throw the need for outward validation into the *flame-filled firepit.*

You long to get back to a version of you that existed before, but what you don't realize is that previous version of you longed to be the person you are today. And the truth is, you will always hold within you every version of yourself at once. You never lost them, you're simply guiding them. You're the soft landing place and the nurturing force they depend on. And your accrued wisdom lights the pathway for all that's still to come, all the future versions of you that you have yet to meet. You are never without them because they are *always within you*.

I love breaking points because they unearth the *strength* that's been hidden within you *all along.*

Self-love will be the needle and thread that sews all your damaged pieces back together—*like a work of art.* These pieces will form a heartfelt quilt, proclaiming a story of *wholeness* and of *choosing a fresh start.*

You can read all the self-help books out there, but please don't forget you hold sacred answers within yourself too. Don't let yourself get so busy on your search for clarity that you disregard your own inherent wisdom. Sometimes getting quiet and checking in with your higher self is the best guidance available to you.

If you have to lose them to find
you—*you lost nothing.*

Never lose your spontaneity. Your unbridled spirit and zest for life. As we get older, we weigh ourselves down and become fearful and complacent. We forget that life is still happening. That getting older is not boring or any descriptor remotely adjacent. We are still little kids in adult bodies, craving our next adventure, in pursuit of lifelong memories we'll always remember.

Sensitivity is a gift to be cherished in a world that overwhelms to the point of numbing and self-preservation. Sensitivity is your *strength*—there is a *blatant correlation.*

When you're a sensitive person, you'll realize that others' strengths may be your weakness, but you will also realize your strengths will be their weakness.

And maybe time alone is just
time to truly figure out *who you are*
when no one else is around.

There's nothing wrong with you.

You are a deep-feeling, messy, complicated, beautiful human being doing your very best to make your way through an *equally* messy, complicated, and beautiful life.

Be gentle with yourself.

There's *nothing* wrong with you.

REST IS
YOUR
BIRTHRIGHT

I know you feel like life is a constant game of catch-up, like you're consistently falling behind or missing the mark each and every time. You set goals with every intention of following through, but your wavering mental health and your tired bones make it feel impossible to pursue—further exacerbating your insecurities and your frustration with yourself, perpetuating an endless loop of shame. You may think you need to be harsher, forcing yourself to just "get it right" while soaking in the blame—but maybe you need the opposite. Maybe you need to honor those calls to rest, to be gentle with yourself, and to stop treating your life like one giant to-do list or test. Your mental health and your well-being are far more important than your status or accomplishments. Move forward at your own pace and in your own natural flow. I promise you the rest will fall into place—like dominos.

—

There is a difference between self-sabotage and needing rest. Please don't confuse the two, *because if you do*, you may convince yourself that your needs are a direct result of something being wrong with you, when in fact, *you are just a human responding to rest cues.*

Inner peace is the new success,
so even when it isn't celebrated,
we cherish it nonetheless.

What if we flipped the societal narrative entirely? I think it's *angelic* how you make time to rest when your body calls for it. I think it's *poetic* how you write in your journal about your daily stresses or your deep-rooted feelings. I think it's *brave* how you continue to heal even though it feels like you are running in place, tending to these same wounds each day. I think your confusion about what you're doing with your life shows you *care*, and that a sense of wonder is the first step toward getting unstuck and guiding you there.

Be motivated and set goals, but don't tie your self-worth to these outcomes. Push yourself out of your comfort zone and try new things, but don't push yourself over the edge. Distance yourself from rigidity by adapting a flexible approach. This will help you learn the difference between bending and breaking. Self-loving and shaming. Flowing and fixating. *This* will be your self-preservation.

Maybe you're not lazy. Maybe you've just been struggling with your mental health for all of these years. Maybe nothing was ever wrong with *you* but wrong with *those who once shamed you.*

You deserve glowing candles, a lo-fi playlist that soothes your soul, an afternoon spent reading for fun, your favorite home-cooked meal, slowing down enough to appreciate the nature that surrounds you, and to recognize *the inherent magic* that lies within you.

Rest. Rest so your nervous system is at peace.

Rest. Rest so you don't have to recover from burnout.

Rest. Rest so you can enjoy the fruits of your labor.

Rest. Rest so you can feel the softness of a slow pace.

Rest. Rest because your soul didn't come to earth with the intention to only work.

Rest. Rest so you can lead by example and teach others how to heal.

I know rest feels counterintuitive when you have so much you want to get done, but trust me when I say not getting sufficient rest *will only hurt you* in the long run. And while it's up to you what can wait versus what's important right now, there is most likely more time for rest *than you ever allow.* I hope you give yourself the downtime your mind body and soul require because *this* will give you the stamina to keep going toward the life you desire. So avoid the crash of nonstop striving. And please stop viewing perfectionism as a form of thriving—when, in fact, it's another form of *self-neglect* and overdriving.

What if birdsong translated to
"relax, it will all be okay"?

When life feels chaotic, seek *simplicity*, seek *stillness*, and seek *shelter* in whatever makes your life feel cozy and safe again.

You don't need to justify your existence through hard work or accolades. You don't need to deplete all of your energy to feel worthy of living. You are safe to experience the slow, soft moments of life. To take notes from nature's pace and quietly excuse yourself from the meaningless race.

When we quiet the constant chatter
in our mind, we can finally listen
to the *whispers* of our heart.

It's okay to take your time in a rushed world. And it is okay to spend time with yourself in a world full of people who are constantly running away from themselves. Let this be a lesson—if you must run, *then run toward yourself*.

Self-care is a daily, honest check-in
met with daily, grace-filled action.

It's okay if you struggle between wanting to live a more goal-oriented, structured life while also wanting to live a slow, soft life. It can be confusing when you want to practice more self-discipline but you also want to be more gentle on yourself. It's a contradicting aspect of the healing journey. But just know that you aren't doing anything wrong by leaning into one or the other. The truth is, our needs are ever-evolving and require us to keep our finger on the pulse. We are not robots; we are human beings just doing our best. So let each day be what it needs to be—*even if that means unrequited rest.*

You are not broken or defective if your energy levels are lower than those around you. Or if the thought of a full social calendar brings you dread because you know it will take days to recharge afterward. You don't need to match the pace of the world around you to be deemed worthy or acceptable. This world wasn't built for a soft soul like yours. So it is your job to build a safe fortress of self-love, protected by your boundaries, in order to maintain your own sense of harmony.

What if life wasn't ever meant to be this busy? And this is why our mental and physical health is crumbling. What if the rising anxiety reports are evidence that we have reached a tipping point in what society expects of us? An audible cry from our minds and bodies to live at a more sustainable pace. A *visceral plea* for change.

.

Slow and gentle living isn't for the weak or the lazy; it's for those who understand that we are not *machines*—for those who grasp the vital human need to integrate *more peace* into our routines.

As much as accomplishing goals can be wildly fulfilling, it can be equally fulfilling to experience something *fun and new*—not to mention, when we are playful and unburdened, we often encounter the most *meaningful breakthroughs.*

If the idea of rest causes you to wrestle with your mind about all that needs to be done, please zoom out and remind yourself that you're on a rock, floating through an infinite universe, rotating the *sun*. Veering from your schedule will *not* cause you to come undone.

What if we viewed rest as productive?
As something we checked off of our list?
Maybe then our needs wouldn't so often be dismissed.

When the world feels like it's spinning too fast and you can't keep up with life's dizzying pace—*slow all the way down*. Stillness is the surest remedy to prevent a future breakdown.

There will be days where you feel on top of the world, and there will be days where you feel ashamed by your lack of progress. *Your worth remains the exact same on both days.*

I know at times it can feel as though the walls are caving in around you, time is escaping you, and you know you require rest but haven't the slightest clue how that would fit into your schedule—*rest anyway.* Schedule it *anyway.* There is no to-do list or goal that is too important to pause. To revisit. To take a breather from. Your health is vital to your success.

What if we didn't question our bodies when they call to us for rest? What if we honored the call with a gentle acceptance—with an understanding that our body has an *intuitive grasp* for what's best? That our inner guidance is stronger than any outside pressure to perform and is certainly not something to suppress.

When all else fails,
don't forget the importance of
deep inhales and deep exhales.

Anytime you can slow down, shut out the noise of the world, and intentionally spend time with yourself—consider that *a win.*

ACTING WITH INTENTIONALITY

You are much more powerful than you realize. Your impact, your choices, your love, your energy—the world would feel your absence if your soul left this planet. You are *needed*, even when it doesn't feel like it. Your life has *meaning*, even if it's not readily apparent to you. And you are *loved*, even when your mind convinces you otherwise.

I used to think I needed a best friend, or a group of them, to feel loved and truly seen. I've since realized I had the potential to be my own best friend all along. Sure, friends are great, but have you ever considered how valuable your own friendship is? You know yourself better than anyone else. You've been there through every up and down over the years. You are always available to you. Keep some of this love and consideration for *yourself*. I promise it will never go to waste. *You* are your foundation. *You* are your rock. Anyone else is extra. But *you*? You got you *for life*. Book the solo trip. Laugh at your own jokes. Treat yourself to new, interesting hobbies. Pursue those dreams. Check in with yourself often, with honesty and compassion. Give yourself the gift of healing. Protect your energy. And remember, *you are the best friend you could ever have.*

It's as equally terrifying as it is empowering when you realize you are the only one who can save yourself in this life. That only *you* can set boundaries and walk away from toxic environments. That only *you* can heal your inner child and nurture that little child inside of you on a daily basis. That only *you* can determine what lights your soul on fire and what fills you with purpose and where your talents come into play. That only *you* can find which habits feel best in your life. That only *you* can figure out how you are going to convince your self-sabotaging tendencies to finally take the back seat while you drive your way to a more fulfilling lifestyle. Despite what's happened on the trajectory of your life, it is *you* who will come to your rescue.

You have to believe you deserve more. And if you don't believe it, you have to dig and dig and reflect on who or what circumstance along the way made you believe you weren't worthy. That you weren't the incredible, magic-filled human you are at your core.

Your future self is providing little hints for what path you should take. These special glimpses come in the form of curiosity, wonder, and intrigue—but we're often so busy self-sabotaging by thinking a better life is out of our league.

Do me this favor: don't ever compare your journey to anyone else's. You may be learning and implementing habits that someone else mastered as a teen. Your accomplishments may feel like someone else's effortless routine. But can I tell you something? Not all roads are paved the same; some are dirt, some are harrowing, and some are flat and newly paved with lanes. *We all traveled to this point with different constraints.*

We often overcomplicate things. If you are tired, *rest*. If you are emotional, *feel*. If you feel stuck, *dig*. If you are lost, *explore*. Don't deprive yourself of solutions, and don't allow your mind to convince you these are signs of failure. These are mere signs of the human existence.

Incorporating new habits is akin to learning how to ride a bike. Terrifying at first, unsettling, and often eliciting a feeling of danger. Then, it slowly starts to feel like your new normal—safe and ordinary. Next thing you know, you are doing these things on autopilot, expending little energy. So don't let your initial fears discourage you out of making the changes that will ultimately transform your life for the better. You deserve to live a life that feels good to you—*a life untethered.*

You can long for an escape to a better life, or you can take action *to make the life you already have better.* You don't need a massive shift to implement improvement in your current situation; You just need to take the beautiful potential that already surrounds you *into consideration.*

Life isn't win or lose; it's a series of
intricate breakthroughs.

You deserve to buy yourself flowers for no reason, to write yourself love notes in your journal, to take yourself on that date or trip you've been wishing to go on—to show up for yourself in all the ways you hope for someone else to. Because at the end of the day, *you deserve your own love too.*

If your life feels like it's in misalignment with who you are, then it's time to get crystal clear on what type of life *does* align with who you are. *You are not stuck.* You are not tethered to misfortune. You are being called to pursue something *new*, leaving behind all of the cognitive distortion.

Change is uncomfortable, until it isn't. New habits seem challenging, until they aren't. A lovely life awaits you—*if only* you are *brave enough* to start.

You have to be ultra-intentional about your self-care, especially if it doesn't come naturally for you. You have to check in with yourself, get creative about solutions, and remember that *you are worthy of your own nurturing.* The world will keep spinning, and you will keep suffering if you don't advocate for your own needs. Give yourself a hug, pour yourself a cup of tea, stretch out your tense limbs, find a quiet space to lie down with zero agenda, tell yourself how strong you are and how amazing you are doing—whatever it is you need, *you have to give it to yourself.* And you have to remember you are worthy enough to *receive it.*

It's normal to not be happy all the time. You were born with a full spectrum of emotions for a reason, and you are meant to experience many contrasting feelings in this lifetime. So the next time you are in the throes of a hard day, remember that the skies won't always be grey.

It's said that at the end of life, people often most regret not living for themselves, not pursuing the dreams planted in their hearts for fear of what others would think. I say we honor them, and breathe life into our dreams boldly, unapologetically, and with respect to our own lives too. So in our last days we can say, *"I lived a life I am proud of because I chose to follow through."*

But this I know to be true: there are stars in the sky, dreams in your heart, love in this world, and flowers to remind you of the undeniable power of a fresh start.

Acknowledge your feelings, your pessimistic thoughts, and your reoccurring fears—but whatever you do, *don't build a home there.* Feel them all, process them, but don't overly scrutinize them. Instead of stockpiling your painful moments, *let them go* and witness the magic of how you transformed your darkest moments into a *radiant glow.*

Your life improves when you learn to appreciate and pour love into the existence that's already in front of you. You decorate your space in a way that both inspires and calms your soul; you clean up the areas you've neglected; you speak kindly to the body you inhabit; you invest in the relationships that feel mutual and healthy; you find books, movies, and hobbies that light something up inside of you; and you learn to admire the pockets of magic in a bird's song or a sorbet sky. Maybe one day you will have more than what you have now, but maybe there's much more to appreciate in this moment than you had ever realized.

Don't let life convince you that it's too late to do something or that you missed your prime years. If you always wanted to study abroad, then study abroad and be relentless in your pursuit. If your style feels scattered and out of touch with who you are, go on a journey of self-discovery and curate a dream wardrobe that speaks to your soul. If you feel as though you lack hobbies, be brave enough to try something new. Because the thing is, you don't have to be born into a certain set of interests or circumstances—you can mold and sculpt your life like your own personal work of art.

The older I get the more I believe the happiest people are the ones who follow their heart and pursue what feels most aligned, bravely throwing caution to the wind in regards to whether it fits the status quo confines.

You deserve warm cups of your favorite coffee or tea. Songs constructed of beautiful melodies with lyrics that feel crafted from the words that would be found in your diaries. Friendships that feel like family and act as a mirror to remind you of your worth. Sunny days with endless birdsong reminding you of the warm embrace from earth. Cozy and nourishing meals to share with your loved ones. Deep, intentional breaths to fill up your lungs. Books that walk you closer home to yourself that you lovingly showcase on your bookshelf. You deserve *a wholesome life.*

Let yourself fall in love with art. Artists. Books. Albums. Cafes. Endearing hobbies. Decorated little corners of your home. But most of all, fall in love with *you* enough to know what lights you up inside and makes this world taste sweet, like honeycomb.

Your anxiety is lying to you. It needs you to gently call it out. It requires you to interrupt its fearful patterns and create new thoughts based in love—building the courage to live out the life you've always dreamed of. You weren't meant to live scared of your shadow, scared of life, and closed off to all of the beauty in this world. You were intended to soak in the magic of this life and, most importantly, to witness that same magic within yourself.

When you find yourself feeling scattered, like you can't find your footing. Drained, like you can't muster the energy to take action. Or uninspired, like you've lost all connection to your passions—remember that you need to do more things that *feed your soul* and do *less things* to please this world.

You'll never be a "fraud" for reinventing yourself. If anything, you'll be a fraud if you pretend to be happy in a life that no longer feels aligned and suited to your authentic self for the sake of pleasing others.

Pay attention to the small moments when you see something you admire and your inner voice automatically proclaims, "I don't have what that requires." There is likely zero evidence to reflect that thought. At any point in time, you have it in you *to switch up the plot.*

You hear about motivational strategies and the importance of pushing yourself, but you don't hear enough about burnout and the importance of rest. How in order to be productive, your inner world can't be overlooked or suppressed.

Fear and self-doubt will cloud your vision entirely. They will convince you that you are stuck, directionless, and hopeless. Fortunately, thoughts are like clouds—moveable and temporary. But you have to intentionally clear them out or they won't move away on their own. You have to take inventory of the very beliefs that are impeding your progress in life. Write them down, question them, disassemble them—and when they try to visit again, view them as unwelcome house guests and kindly show them the door.

It's uncomfortable before it's easy, but if you never make any changes, discomfort will be present due to your stagnancy. Decide what you want in your life, expect the transitions to be challenging, but remind yourself: it will soon be easy and you won't even realize it's happening.

TRUSTING
YOUR LIFE'S
TIMING & FLOW

You Deserve Your Own Love Too

I want you to know it's okay to feel like you are taking one step forward and two steps back. I know this causes you anxiety, fear, and confusion. You feel like you're running in place, or swimming through mud—but can I tell you this? Life is a weird dance, and those steps can't be quantified in simple mathematical terms. That one step could have been a giant leap for you, for your healing, for your own soul growth. And those two steps back could have been miniscule in comparison. So keep going, embrace the weird flow of life, and trust that your efforts are never in vain.

Will you do me a favor? Don't compare your productivity to anyone else's. You are no less than someone who accomplishes more.

On the days where you feel like a failure because you can't seem to keep up with your to-do list, I hope you know you are no less valuable and you are free to *simply exist*.

Depression is the ultimate gaslighter, leading us to believe we will always feel down, that we are perpetually unworthy, and that life is nothing but a challenge—but this is entirely untrue. Let the storm pass through, and remember, *your life carries so much magic and beauty too.*

The people you look up to struggle too. Don't be fooled by *a carefully curated culture.*

There is an undeniable peace that comes with *surrendering* the need to know how everything plays out in your life. You clear out the debris of fear and create space for the beauty of what's in front of you now. You give life the chance to surprise you, to instill some magic and hope in the unseen. You relinquish the illusion of power and ultimately trade it in for more than you could *ever dream*.

We are big proponents of to-do lists, but what about creating a list each night to reflect on our accomplishments? Some of these can be as simple as, "I fed myself a nourishing meal," "I went for a walk," "I journaled my difficult feelings." What might be considered a small win for you one day could be a huge accomplishment for you another day. *Meet yourself* where you are. *Love on yourself* where you are. *Celebrate yourself* where you are.

There will be moments in life where you will feel utterly powerless over your struggles. You'll get up each day and fight the good fight, yet there will only be so much that is in your control. These seasons will require you to straddle the fine line of putting fourth concerted effort to improve your situation, and trust falling completely, with an understanding that the universe will catch you with open arms.

Instead of wishing for more, ask yourself how you can make the most of what you already have in this very moment. People think *more* will solve their problems, but oftentimes their problems are still there to greet them when they get there. Lean into the small, magical, seemingly mundane moments of right now. See the opportunity in what already exists, and build from a place of contentment, letting gratitude persist.

I know you are hopeful and fearful all at once. Confused and tired with little bursts of energy. I want to remind you that no matter how hard it feels right now, this isn't how your story ends. One day you're going to think back to these times right now and you're going to say, *"I made it."*

It's been said that what's not working out for you is often a protection or a redirection—a sign from the universe that says "not yet." I know it can feel soul-crushing to work so hard for something and not see the fruits of your labor. I know it can feel like the whole world is conspiring against you, and that this is just your lot in life—to struggle. But please remember the delay is never a punishment, or a measure of your worth, and it's certainly not a predictor of your destiny. There are pieces of your story that will make more sense as time unfolds. For now, you have to trust the yield signs in your path and press forward with an open mind and patient heart. *There is so much more to come.*

Don't let the hard times derail you.
Feel your feelings.
Reassess your course.
Adjust your plans accordingly.
And remember, *you are a resilient force.*

And then there you are as a gust of warm wind wrestles the trees around you in just a way that calms your soul. A bridge of a song raises the tiny hairs on your arms in awe. A stranger smiles at you in a way that makes you feel safe in this world. You take a bite of your favorite fruit and can feel your cells singing from the nourishment. You look over at a friend and burst into laughter at the same moment. A monarch butterfly graces your path, and you can't help but stop and admire its beauty. For a brief moment, life feels like it makes sense. All the struggle feels nonexistent. *You can see the glimmers of light again.*

What if we come to earth to enjoy the magic of nature, to laugh and play, to love, to hurt, to heal, to learn— to live life in all its complexity? What if it's meant to feel good, bad, enchanting, and everything in between? What if you aren't doing a single thing wrong? In fact, what if *this* is exactly what you came here to experience? Would it change how you see yourself, your struggles, and your current situation?

Don't let the hard days give you tunnel vision.
There are plenty of beautiful days ahead of you.
There will be love, laughter, and glimmers of
hope too. Struggle won't always be in your view.

Each day you need to meet yourself where you're at. Emotionally and energetically. Your needs will change—and that's to be expected. But instead of punishing yourself with shame-filled circular thoughts, meet yourself with tender compassion. *Be your own safe haven.*

Your mental health may *ebb and flow*,
but your worth remains the same.

When the night falls and the hard days settle into your bones, leaving you to feel helpless and hopeless—please remind yourself of the healing power of a good night's sleep. Tomorrow won't feel so dreary. This heavy feeling is *temporary*.

Please don't compare your progress to anyone else's. It's said that Leonardo da Vinci's *Mona Lisa* took upwards of fifteen years to paint while Van Gogh's *Starry Night* is suspected to have been completed in a matter of a few moonlit nights. You wouldn't compare the two. You wouldn't because they're both valuable and respectable in their own right. Both artists surely fought through and encountered their own plight—yet both paintings beam with undeniable beauty in their unique light.

Don't let the gap between where you are and where you'd like to be convince you that you are a failure, or somehow not capable of those dreams planted in your heart. At the beginning of any journey, there will be powerful shifts occurring that will be invisible to the naked eye. Much like a flower bulb beneath the soil, breaking, sprouting, and establishing roots in preparation for what's to come—your progress bares roots *you will soon blossom from.* You will witness small bursts of progress on your journey without realizing the magnitude buried deep inside. Until one day, those small bursts will become tidal waves, and all the shrouded mystery will subside. That slow and steady journey was not a product of shortcomings or missteps; it was a healthy evolution built on a foundation of integrity, one that surely no one ever suspects.

It's okay to be
Happy and hurting
Hopeful and scared
Self-aware and confused
Confident and insecure.
It's okay to be human,
wildly complex to your core.

Get in the habit of asking yourself what you need right now. This world will suck you up and consume all of your time if you let it. It's up to you to slow down, get clear on what you need, and determine what is unfit.

I know it feels like people are running laps around you—when you are already unsure of why your life feels stagnant. It can become quite easy to feel as though something is wrong with you, or you're somehow undeserving of good things. But life isn't a race, and it's not a competition to be had. Free yourself and get off the race track entirely—expand. Go to the forest, or the garden, or the ocean and let it remind you that the only thing you need to do is to listen to your own internal guidance system, forging your own pace, bathing in your own inherent wisdom.

We can't outrun struggle, heartbreak, or grief. These experiences are intricately woven into the human experience for every soul on earth. But there is also joy, ease, unconditional love, and hope. Hang on tight in the hard times and bask in the good times. *You were designed to experience it all.*

THE BEAUTY IN YOUR HEALING JOURNEY

You Deserve Your Own Love Too

134 | CHELSEY ARMFIELD

The goal for this year is a healed nervous system, a calm mind, a passionate heart, a loved inner child, and a balanced life.

People say healing is lifelong, and to some degree this is true. But the messy, ugly, all-encompassing healing? This won't always belong to you. Yes, there will come a point where your trauma visits you in momentary stings or crying spells, or where you notice yourself slipping back into an old destructive pattern you thought you had conquered, or where you have to grieve the life of someone you truly honored. But the healing you are doing now? It is carrying you to safer pastures where the pain visits but does not reside. The healing you are doing now isn't for nothing, and the depths of your pain will surely subside.

And sometimes healing looks like doing *nothing* other than accepting yourself *exactly as you are today.*

Healing is like going on a road trip with no navigation system or any tangible inclination of where you are going—you are simply trying to find yourself, to know yourself, and to love yourself a little more than yesterday.

You may not know how to feel better all at once—the special recipe to your healing. But you will start to pay attention to what feels good and to gently question what doesn't. You will start to reflect on the type of life you want to live, and map out plans for how to get there. You will have moments of failure, and you will heal each time you respond to your shortcomings with compassion. You will have seasons of rest, of going within, and you will have seasons filled with inspirational bursts of energy. You will go into hermit mode, and you will shut out the world so you can finally hear your own voice. You will have seasons of intentional friendship and feeling rooted in connections that soothe your soul. You will learn your likes and dislikes and try on new hobbies for size. You will catch yourself singing in the shower, reading more books, and finding solace in your journal. You will learn how to calm your nervous system and self-regulate when times get tough. Most importantly, you will learn a sacred truth: you have *always* been enough.

Your mental health isn't something to put on the back burner. It should be something you monitor, foster, and nurture throughout every season of your life. This doesn't mean your mental health will always be in a good place, but it *does* mean you will always be there to lovingly greet it and gently work through it.

Depression is like being trapped in a glass box without a key. You desperately long to escape it and join the rest of the world, but no matter what you seem to do, you are separated by a thick glass fogging your vision. You don't know how you got in there, how to break out of it, or how long you will be trapped inside—but you do know you've felt this way before, so you trust with time you will find your way out again. And sometimes that inner-knowing is the only flotation device that carries us through. So *we wait and we wait* until we feel as good *as new.*

We are taught so much in school, but what if we learned how to regulate our nervous systems, how to express our feelings, how to believe in ourselves, and how to listen to our inner guidance systems? *Imagine how different this world would be.*

A butterfly is a brilliant reminder that even when we heal and transform, we will still encounter adversity. The butterfly still faces predators and dangers in this world. The only difference? *Now it can take flight.*

You know what makes you inspiring? That you never gave up in circumstances that you had every right to. That you chose to heal and see it through. That you faced your shadow self and chose to love her all the same. That you knit a quilt of purpose out of your struggle and pain. Building a life from scratch that most others will never be brave enough to obtain.

And sometimes your healing will
ask you to take several steps
backward so you can travel leaps
and bounds *forward.*

You want to know who truly loves you for you? Go on a healing journey and see who's still around through it all—who didn't check out but *checked in* and cared enough to meet you where you are.

Sometimes the bravest thing you can do is let go of what hurt you. Trusting that you are safe to move on. Opening your arms to all of the new loving experiences to come.

A crucial step of healing is hanging up your victimhood and stepping into your power. You didn't deserve what happened to you, but you do deserve a life full of confidence and joy. You deserve to see just how resilient you are and always have been. You deserve to see how the universe is working to support you, not punish you. You deserve a fresh beginning, free of the weight that has been crushing your spirit *for far too long.*

You are worthy of clarity,
consistency, and people who
make conscious decisions
to protect your heart.

You impress me. How you keep going and keep fighting these invisible battles on a daily basis. How you manage to make time for your personal growth in the midst of this quiet daily tug of war within yourself—I'm rooting for you. I know it has taken *everything in you* to keep going.

There will come a point in your life where you are indifferent to those who hurt you. You won't feel mad anymore. You won't feel tearful anymore. You won't have that gnawing feeling within you that you need closure or validation for all the suffering it caused you. Instead, you will feel a detachment from them entirely. *Until then*, feel what you need to feel because one day, these memories won't hold so much power over you. They will feel distant, *like someone else's story.*

Healing is when you slowly demolish your harmful habits and conditioning, slay the dragons of self-doubt, and build a castle on soil comprised of self-love, with a moat constructed of boundaries to protect your energy—a great transitioning. *A labor of love.*

I know it can be hard to pursue new things when you don't even feel safe in your own body in your day-to-day life. The shallow breaths you take, the clenched jaw, the knotted shoulders, the rumination and worry, the self-limiting beliefs, and the undeniable fatigue born from it all. Maybe the only goal to pursue in this moment is proving to your body *you are safe now.* Create a journal practice, slow it all down, stretch your tired limbs, focus on nothing but your breath, admire nature's stillness and beauty, listen to music that soothes your soul and quiets your mind, hydrate and nourish your body. Most of all, lean into the fundamentals of nervous-system regulation. You deserve to feel at home in your body, and not like a lost stranger roaming the halls.

Never underestimate the healing power of jumping into a cold lake on a warm summer night, taking a scenic drive during sunset just because, full-body dancing in your kitchen when no one is home, cuddling up and watching an old film, or lying on the floor to do nothing but daydream about your future.

I hope that one day I find someone who is as loving and loyal as you pretended to be. But for now, *I'm grateful I have me.*

Growing older is getting to know yourself
deeper, and knowing yourself deeper will help
you love yourself more tender. Heal into the
currents of aging, and allow yourself to drift
your way back home to yourself.

How do you heal?

Shadow work, inner-child healing,
nervous-system regulation.

How do you heal?

Laughter, rest, admiring the sunset,
discovering new hobbies.

(Your healing will look different day by day)

There's just something about a person who can make it through the thick of their healing, through their loneliest season, through all of the uncertainty, and who manages to come out the other side. This person develops an unshakable sense of self and unlocks a rare level of self-empowerment. This person is a precious gem in human form.

Journal. Let your emotions explode out of you and onto the page in front of you. Feel the release of letting go of what has been caged in your heart for far too long, and free yourself from the hurt that was never yours to carry. By doing this, you hold a ceremony, one where your trauma can now exit your body and finally lay buried.

Dig up your trauma,
clear out the soil,
and then plant lilacs and lilies at your feet.
Trade in your pain and enjoy this new space of retreat.

And then one day you wake up and you realize that you never actually needed them—you needed *you*.

This stage of my healing is less about grieving my past and more about welcoming in my future. Who do I want to be? How do I want to show up? How can I build new habits upon a foundation of self-love?

I don't know who needs this gentle reminder, but you are still lovable when you are upset and hurting, or when your life feels like a mess—you are still lovable in all your broken-down distress.

There are days where your cup will run on empty and your spirit will be zapped. Days where you will feel overcome with a thick cloud of emotion blocking your path. Days where you will feel like a stranger inhabiting your own skin. And days where it will feel impossible to win. The solutions may not always be clear, but trust me when I say, better days *are much closer than they appear.*

People don't talk enough about how exhausting it is to battle with your mental health. When so much of your energy goes into feeling "normal," you have little left inside of you to apply to anything else. This is further proof why you shouldn't compare your life to anyone else's, and why you need to remember to celebrate the small wins too. Though invisible to the outside world, never shame yourself for what you are going through.

We preach rest, but we don't teach how to combat the hypervigilance so that we can do so adequately. We preach talk therapy, but we don't talk about somatic healing and how the trauma lives inside of us on a physical level. We preach healthy connection and community, but we don't account for the difficulty in building new relationships from scratch. There are several layers to your healing, to undoing, and to reconstructing your life from the ground up.

Healing is choosing to remodel your inner world. Clearing out the ghosts that haunt you, the fears that impair you, and the lies that smother you. It's opening up the windows and shutters and letting in the breeze and sunrays. It's a reclaiming of the home that has always been yours. Creating a safe place for you to spend your days.

I know it doesn't feel like it right now, but there will be a time in your near future when you will be moving through your day and you will realize you don't feel that same weight of your trauma anymore. You will feel light again, like you did before the hurt. You will feel freedom from those who harmed you, and they will seem entirely insignificant to you in this wholesome new life you've built. The wisdom will remain, but it will feel like someone else's story because the pain won't feel so personal anymore. And it's true: it was never personal. It was never about you. You were just an innocent bystander in the wrong place at the wrong time—if not you, it would have been someone else. You will simply return to sender.

There comes a point in your healing where you need to reconcile and fuse your resilience with the softness you've so bravely cultivated. It may feel like you're on shaky ground, like one diminishes or compromises the other, but it's quite the opposite—one protects the other. They'll hold hands and guide you to where you're going.

Healing is a misleading feeling because you often have to unravel before you can weave a new path. You have to enter the dusty dark attic of your mind, clear out the cobwebs, and scrub the floorboards. You have to turn yourself inside out and learn to love and accept every little piece within you. The very things you hid from: the pain, the programming, the denial—all of it. But one day, there will be no more dark, dusty attic, no more secrets from yourself. There is a fresh start—a lighter and brighter path *glimmering* with hope.

Maybe there isn't a day where you are fully healed—but maybe you have days where warm, proud tears roll down your cheeks, when you realize just how far you've come. And days where you realize what used to be a struggle for you is now blissful and routine. And days where you identify your inner critic before the thought resonates and replace it with a kind thought instead. And days where you feel confident in situations that used to terrify you to your core. There are several measures of progress on your healing and self-love journey. Don't get caught up in the idea that it won't ever feel better. I promise you if you stay the course, you will enter greener pastures, and *you will feel a wholeness within* that you never knew.

Loving yourself is a *homecoming*.
Every fiber of your being has been
awaiting your return.

Welcome home.

C H E L S E Y   A R M F I E L D was born and raised in Washington State, just outside of Seattle, and currently resides there with her husband and dog. She graduated from the University of Washington with a bachelor's degree in Media Communications, with a focus on journalism. She has ultimately discovered her true passion lies in self-love advocacy and writing. Her writing is inspired from real-life experiences, which have without a doubt shaped her path, while also providing valuable life lessons. She feels passionate about sharing this wisdom with others so they, too, can heal through self-love and go onto live out their fullest life. For more books and for social media information visit: C H E L S E Y A R M F I E L D . C O M

MORE BOOKS FROM
CHELSEY ARMFIELD

Heal to Glow
Poetry & Prose

The Real Glow Up
Self-help Memoir

Available for purchase at:

CHELSEYARMFIELD.COM

Made in United States
North Haven, CT
15 September 2024

57430906R00114